RISE UP,
MAMAS!

*How to Step Into Your Power
as a Parent During a World Crisis*

RISE UP, MAMAS!

*How to Step Into Your Power
as a Parent During a World Crisis*

Traci Sanders

Fresh Ink Group
Guntersville

Rise Up, Mamas!
How to Step into Your Power
as a Parent During a World Crisis

Fresh Ink Group
An Imprint of:
The Fresh Ink Group, LLC
1021 Blount Avenue #931
Guntersville, AL 35976
Email: info@FreshInkGroup.com
FreshInkGroup.com

Edition 1.0   2020
Edition 2.0   2020

Front Cover by Traci Sanders
Book design by Amit Dey / FIG
Covers by Stephen Geez / FIG
Editorial Proof by Beth Hale
Associate publisher Lauren A. Smith / FIG

The author's intent in providing this book is to offer practical tips and
strategies based upon personal life experience and this advice is not in
any way meant to be considered medical or scientific.

Cataloging-in-Publication Recommendations:
FAM034000   **FAMILY & RELATIONSHIPS** / Parenting / General
REF031000   **REFERENCE** / Survival & Emergency Preparedness
REF015000   **REFERENCE** / Personal & Practical Guides

Library of Congress Control Number: 2020909215

ISBN-13: 978-1-947893-02-3 Papercover
ISBN-13: 978-1-947893-03-0 Hardcover
ISBN-13: 978-1-947893-04-7 Ebooks

Table of Contents

Introduction

I want to preface this book by stating that I am not a family therapist, a mindset guru, or a doctor. The tips and strategies I offer in this book are based on my personal experience as a mom, wife, and an educator of young children for more than a decade. I don't claim anything in this book to be medical advice, just effective strategies I've used in my own life. I'm not sharing this as the be-all-end-all of parenting, marriage, or business advice. However, as an author and business woman, I know the power of sharing one's story. I truly believe that there has never been a more perfect time to not only share our stories to let people know where we've come from, but to share our journeys, to let them know where we're going. This is my story.

I've been a work-at-home mom in different capacities since my first child (now 22) was around two years of age. My first work-at-home experience was as a dispatcher for a cable company, where I had a Nextel radio (raise your hand if you're feeling old now because you know what this is) attached to my hip nearly 24/7. When I lost that job, due to the owner retiring out of the blue one day, I frantically began looking for another job. Our boys were six and four at that time, and I knew we couldn't afford childcare for both, so I needed to find something to do from home again. My solution was to open a daycare center in my home. It turned out to be the biggest blessing to our family in many ways. Not only did it provide a substantial income for me, it taught me a great deal about human behavior that I have been able to apply to my own life multiple times. I closed down my center and retired when my youngest child was going into middle school because I wanted to be more present with my own kids. They were doing online school at the time, so I wanted to be more available to help them with their schooling as well.

I share this story to let you know that I've always been my children's first teacher. Even though I worked from home, I made sure to educate my children and impart life skills to prepare them for the real world. I always saw myself as their most important influence, even to the point of what some would call sheltering or being overprotective. But I didn't care what other people thought of my methods. I took my role as a parent very seriously.

Now, I get that not every mama desires to stay home and educate their children, much less anyone else's. I didn't think I was built for it either in the beginning. I was already stretched to the max with the daycare kids. We had found our daily rhythm, and I was not looking forward to that changing. But I also didn't like feeling out of touch with my own kids' educational experience. So, my husband and I decided to enroll them in online school and thus began our journey.

I pretty much fumbled through our first year, even though I can't count how many times people said to me, "I don't know how you do it all." The ironic thing is I never felt like I was any type of superhero or that I was doing anything special. I simply considered it my duty to be my children's main influence. The truth is, a lot of things change when we become parents. We can't always control what our path is going to look like or how our lives are going to play out.

As I'm penning this book, we as a society are experiencing an invisible enemy, a virus that is sweeping the entire world, causing numerous health attacks and deaths. My beloved dream country, Italy, has suffered tens of thousands of fatalities. None of us could have ever predicted a situation of this magnitude. It's not just affecting our home state or country. It's a world-wide pandemic that is touching lives with no regard to race, gender, age, religion, social status, or occupation. Restaurants have closed down or transitioned to pick-up only. Churches and schools have moved to online participation. Major sports events and concerts have been cancelled for the foreseeable future. Basic necessities like toilet paper, hand soaps, and cleaning products have been cleared from the shelves and consumers are in a panic, hoarding these items out of fear or a scarcity mindset.

Manual-labor-based employees like hairstylists, makeup artists, and massage therapists are scrambling to find ways to digitize their services and salvage their businesses. Yes, it reads more like a science-fiction novel than real life, but it's the reality we're facing right now.

But there is a bright side. It's been centuries since our society has experienced such a level of people bonding with their families, reconnecting with friends, businesses and individuals reaching out to support their community by offering their skills or facilities to create necessary items like gloves and masks to protect our essential workers. Yes, only certain people have been given passes to work during this time, and have been deemed essential in this crisis.

What it all comes down to is that we all are being nudged into new situations. Parents are being forced to take an active role in their children's social life and education. Businesses are being forced to focus on and value their existing customers like never before. Church-goers are realizing the power of their faith and relationship with God, not just their church building or church family. Basically, our world is being forced to pivot.

x | *Rise Up, Mamas!*

This shift is bringing resistance, anxiety, trepidation, and uncertainty for those who aren't embracing it. But for those who are willing to become a bit vulnerable and creative, stay open to new ideas and ways of doing things, whether in this situation or any future crisis, this can become one of the most impactful, fulfilling, and memorable moments in our lives.

My goal in writing this book is to offer hope, insight, and strategies to guide my fellow mamas through this new world we're experiencing and help you come out better and stronger than ever on the other side. I hope to inspire you to not only step into the role of your child's ever-present parent and teacher during this crisis, but to embrace the journey and become your child's greatest influence in their life, as it should be.

This is your moment to become your child's hero. They are watching to see how you handle this situation. Will you crumble and complain or rise and reclaim or reinvent yourself?

This book is not for those who wish to "ride out this wave" or stick their head in the sand and pretend this is just a bad dream or that things will go back to normal soon enough. It's not going to resonate with those who are looking for someone to blame for their pain or struggles. In fact, it will probably annoy you more than help you, if you're not open to options or solutions.

However, if you're ready for change, ready to learn something new, and ready to step into your potential and discover your power as a parent, then keep reading. I urge you to buckle up because there will be some bumps along the way. But one thing is certain: you will never forget this ride, and neither will your children.

Chapter 1

Accepting the Shift

As I write this, the world has been on lockdown for almost a month now. Essential businesses are the only ones thriving. Others are merely surviving. A federal mandate of "no groups more than ten" is in place, and some areas even have implemented curfews or police-escorted shopping experiences in stores. It's definitely a different world, and this is just starting to sink in for some people.

Most schools and daycare centers are shut down, with classes and programs being offered online wherever possible. Teachers have been scrambling for weeks to assemble curriculum, work through technical issues, and stay connected virtually to their students.

For the most part, parents are "finding their grooves" when it comes to online schooling. My children have been doing online school for years, so I'm quite thankful we aren't being forced to transition to that amidst the chaos right now. Our first year was definitely a learning curve for all of us.

Homeschooling has become more and more prevalent over the past decade, due to an increase in work-from-home opportunities. However, what the students are navigating to during this shift is not a true homeschooling experience. Authentic homeschool curriculum involves a great deal of planning, implementing hands-on learning experiences, and improvising when needed. Public school students have been thrown into an online-only classroom, essentially. Their teachers and administrators had little time to prepare themselves or their students academically or emotionally for such a transition. Many families don't even have internet or computers for their children to use in completing their work. As well, many parents are now working from home, trying to balance everything out day to day, or stressing about being laid off and losing money for the household. These are not the issues that typically go along with transitioning to a home-based learning experience, or at least in such a hurried fashion. I definitely don't envy the teachers, school administrators, or parents of these children during this chaos. My heart goes out to all of them.

Alas, here we are. This is what most families' daily lives look like now. The routine is no more. Having a reason to get up at a certain time or dress a certain way is not a concern for many. It would be so easy to slide into a haphazard existence right now, throw in the towel and say, "What's the use? We only have a few more weeks of school anyway." This is certainly what may be going through the heads of many children right now, or coming out of their mouths. That's why it's crucial that we step into our power as parents and keep our kids focused and moving forward. We must set the example of how to not only survive this crisis but thrive and grow through it. This *must* serve a purpose of some kind in our lives. We must learn something and evolve from it, or else it was just another catastrophe that took place, when it's all over.

Each of us is dealing with this situation in our own way. It's somewhat of a grieving process, and not just mourning the deaths of our friends and loved ones. Some of us are saying goodbye to our comfortable, convenient way of life. Our favorite restaurants and beauty salons. Our ability to simply walk into a store at any time we choose and find what we're looking for. Our freedom to get in our cars and drive to see whomever we want when the mood strikes. Our confidence and security of knowing we have a job to go to every day. We're grieving the loss of the familiar, our identities, our passions, and our basic freedoms. The world is in a highly emotional state, and some will take longer than others to get through it. Some may never fully make that transition. Regardless if we embrace it or not, one thing is certain: the world has changed and will keep changing. But that's okay. Not all change is bad.

The first step in moving forward and healing is acceptance. We must come to the realization that the world as we knew it, has changed. We *will* get through this, but nothing will ever be the same again. Pretending this isn't happening or that things will "go back to normal soon" is like trying to unwrite a song. It's already been written. The words exist. Now all we can do is bump along to a new soundtrack we've created in this world. Now is not a time to "sit this one out" and wait for your favorite song to come back on. I, for one, intend to dance, no matter what tune is playing.

Once you've accepted the reality of the situation, you can move forward in dealing with it and can set up yourself and your family for success.

Chapter 2

Get Set Up for Success

Whether today is your Day 1 or Day 31 of impact due to the quarantine, you can start fresh and get your household set up to thrive from this point forward.

While I do feel that a routine is an important part of success in this, I'm not of the mindset that the routine or schedule has to mirror that of public school, or even be rigid for that matter. I *do* feel that some basic principles are crucial to have in place. It's important to get up, get dressed—not just hang out in your pajamas all day—shower and groom yourself every day. Don't skip over mirrors during this time. It's vital that you see yourself every day, to keep things in perspective.

One thing I'll suggest is to wake your child up around the same time every day and encourage them to go to bed around the same time every evening. Try to keep meals around the same time each day as well to provide some constants for your children, especially younger ones. Eat meals together, especially breakfast, because it sets the tone for the entire day. Children of all ages need structure, but younger ones in particular. Remember, this doesn't mean your child has to get up at the crack of dawn like before, nor does it mean you should allow them to sleep into until noon. Between 8 a.m. and 9 a.m. is usually a happy medium. You know your child best. This also depends on what time your child's online lessons begin. That's something to keep in mind as well.

It's also a good idea to look at a calendar every day. During quarantine, it can be easy to lose track of time and days. Stay focused and on track by looking at your calendar every day. In fact, and even better idea would be to look at your calendar the night before, to plan out your schedule for the following day. Write down a few must-dos for your child's schoolwork and your personal tasks or goals for the day. I'd encourage you, as the parent, to have at least *one* goal to work toward every day. This sets a good example for your kids to see you staying productive. If you have a home-based business or remote job, this should be no problem, but even if you don't, come up with one chore, task, or activity you can work on each day.

Another thing you might want to consider is providing a "school zone" and/or "work zone" for you and your kids. Each child will need their own laptop or device to work from, if possible. If not, you'll need to set up a schedule so each person can get their work done in a timely manner. It's a good idea to also set a schedule that everyone adheres to. Perhaps even set a timer to help transition everyone into the next phase of the day.

If you are working from home and must be on the phone or Zoom calls during specific times, be sure to put that on the schedule. Let your children know ahead of time so they don't disturb you. You might even consider placing a ribbon on your office door as a "do not disturb" signal.

The school or work zone should be distraction free—no music, television, family happenings, etc. during work time. If you place your child (or yourself) too close to the kitchen, there may be a desire to snack all day. If your child is in their bedroom, there may be a temptation to get too comfy or even fall asleep, or perhaps get distracted by music or other websites non-school related. Yes, music can be a distraction if your child is spending too much time "getting ready to get ready" by creating song playlists, watching a quick video, or listening to a favorite song. It's better to have instrumental music playing, if any, because it takes time and energy to focus on lyrics, which detracts from the material at hand that needs to be processed.

I would also suggest taking phones away during school time. It's just too much of a distraction or temptation. Your child can receive their phone back during breaks or when their assignments are completed for the day.

It might help your child by providing him or her with a planner as well. This builds confidence in taking responsibility in their schedule, helps them stay on track with assignments, and gives them a sense of control in the process. Not to mention, it feels good to be able to *see* progress in action and physically check off tasks.

Be aware that if you place your child beside a window or outside to work, distractions may present themselves as well. They may become engrossed in an animal playing in the yard or other child passing by or an activity going on across the street. Even something as simple as strong weather can slow a child down, such as a gloomy, rainy day, and cause a child to feel lethargic or sleepy.

Get your child into the habit of having all the necessary tools for each assignment before they begin. Pens, pencils, class notebooks to take notes are just to name a few. Since the work is being completed online, you probably won't have textbooks or workbooks to deal with. But note-taking can be very helpful to navigate and understand lessons.

Make sure your child's laptop is charged each night or you have the charger handy. It's best to unplug the charger from the device and wall once it's fully charged. Overheating can result from overcharging. It's a good idea to have a cooling pad or a laptop with a built-in fan to help prevent overheating.

Okay, so you've gotten up and dressed, you've got your designated work/school space set up, you've got your schedule and goals written down, you've got the distractions minimized, and you've got the tools needed for the process. Now you're ready to get started on your first day of school (and work) at home. Let the adventure begin.

Chapter 3

Zooming Through Your Day

Most schools and businesses have opted to utilize Zoom as the primary online communication tool. Skype, Messenger, Google Hangouts, and Apple Face Time are still available for casual video conversations, but Zoom has become the preferred method, so this chapter is focused on some aspects of setting up Zoom and using it safely because, while being able to video chat with teachers and fellow classmates can be fun and can take the sting out of social distancing, it's also important to remember that the good guys aren't the only ones using this platform. Online predators are hacking into these Zoom calls and soliciting to kids. Therefore, a few guidelines need to be put in place for your kids' safety when using Zoom, especially the younger ones.

1. Since Zoom is a video-based tool, it's important to be able to see what and who your kids are looking at and interacting with at all times. Set up your kids to work within your view.

2. Children should NOT be on Zoom in their bedrooms or in a room with a closed door.

3. Children should be fully dressed when on Zoom. (i.e. teen girls need to be wearing a bra and a shirt that covers cleavage and such)

4. Children should NEVER join a meeting or accept a request from someone you don't know. Check out the privacy settings. You'd be surprised at some of the defaults. Adjust them as needed.

5. When your child joins a Zoom call, initially get them to join without video or audio. These features can be activated as needed during the call. Truly, kids should not have video on unless required by their teachers.

6. Try to avoid providing personal, identifying information and NEVER allow your child to share these details verbally or in the chat with someone you don't know.

7. Just like with bedrooms, do not allow phones or other devices to be taken into the bathroom as well, especially when on Zoom.

8. Tell your child to let you know immediately if someone strange tries to talk to them or if they see something strange pop up in a video or image while on Zoom.

9. Keep Zoom calls to a limited amount of time. Thirty-to-forty-minute sessions should suffice.

Now that we've discussed some safety aspects of Zoom, here are a few tactical tips and tricks:

1. Download the Zoom for free at www.zoom.us/download

2. It's a good idea to allow your child to simply join a Zoom meeting as requested by their teacher rather than have his

or her own account set up. Don't give your child your login details for your account. You don't want your child to have free access. You can also choose "view in browser" rather than downloading the app.

3. Before you start a Zoom session, you'll want to test the app by visiting www.zoom.us/test and click "join" and open to launch it. Once you're in the Zoom room, you can right click on the microphone to test the audio and the same process to test the camera. Again, you can also join in a browser.

4. Once your child is in Zoom, he or she may be able to share their screen, chat with other participants, etc. Again, keep an eye on this activity. Your child should only use chat if needed, to minimize distractions. The teacher will most likely deactivate chat until needed during the lesson.

5. Your child can also take screenshots of the session. The process depends on what device is being used to access Zoom.

6. Your child can raise their hand during the lesson to ask a question by clicking on the appropriate icon under the "participants" feature.

7. If or when the teacher asks your child to share their screen, this can be done by clicking on the green "share" button.

Those are just a few quick tips on using Zoom for learning. You can also use it as a general video chat tool to communicate with friends or loved ones, if you open your own free account at www.zoom.us. If you keep the calls under forty minutes, there is no charge.

It's very important that you and your child know that Zoom has its own audio and video features, so just because you turn off your sound or video on your actual device does not mean the Zoom participants can no longer see or hear you. They can! So, you control your audio and video through Zoom, not your device. It's always best to end a Zoom meeting completely and make sure the app is closed down when your session ends. In fact, it's probably a good idea to keep your device camera covered at all times when in use on internet, just for general safety, especially for younger kids.

Zoom is a great tool when implemented correctly, but as with anything internet-based, safety comes first.

Chapter 4

Learning with Littles

Many moms are struggling with two things when it comes to their younger kids: 1. How to keep them engaged and learning. 2. How to keep them occupied while Mommy is working or helping older children with their school work.

Let me just say that I've been there! I had a full daycare when I first started online school with my three kids, who, at the time were sixteen, fourteen, and eight. So, I had to get very creative with keeping the daycare kids entertained and learning while also overseeing my kids' school work. (Oops, is my cape showing again?) Just kidding. I'm *no* superhero, as I've said before. I just got really good at time management, planning, and thinking outside the box.

Here are 19 Hands-on Activities little ones can do while you're working or helping your older kids with their tasks:

1. Dry pasta with scoops, spoons, bowls, etc. for pouring and measuring. Not much mess and they are learning math concepts.

2. Dry oatmeal or rice in a shallow pan – practicing writing letters or drawing shapes. Small motor skills.

3. Shaving cream on the kitchen table. Give them large sponges in various shapes to make prints. By the time you're done with helping your older kids, the sponges will have soaked up the shaving cream and you simply need to wipe down your child with a wet cloth. They will be entertained, clean, and smelling good!

4. Soft pom poms and plastic tongs. Let your child pick up the items using just the tongs. They can also go through the house seeing what else they can pick up using just the tongs. Kids LOVE tongs, by the way. This works on fine motor skills and hand-eye coordination. Not everything they learn has to be academic.

5. Tape one end of a piece of yarn or string to the table. Give your child large beads or Fruit Loops to slide onto the string to create a necklace or bracelet. Snack and math combined. I call it Snack-ademia!

6. Give your child a large brown box and some crayons. Let them color (decorate) the box as desired. When finished, cut out a door and windows to make a playhouse.

7. Give your child a small, round laundry basket and either rolled-up socks or balls of paper to toss into it.

8. Draw pictures (or write words for older kids) of 20-30 items in your home that he or she can collect in a basket. Kids love scavenger hunts. This works on team-building skills and problem-solving skills.

9. You can always do school outside with your older ones while the younger ones have a bike wash, paint the fence with water, go through an obstacle course, play on the playground or in the sandbox.

10. Hide plastic eggs for your young ones to find. It doesn't just have to happen at Easter.

11. Give your little one a bucket to collect nature items outside – acorns, pinecones, leaves, etc. Just be sure to supervise the area for hazards.

12. Let your little one draw on the driveway with chalk.

13. Give your child a pile of Tupperware lids and containers, and ask them to match the sets.

14. Teach your child colors by giving them colored Post-its to go around the house and stick to objects that correspond to those colors.

15. Put painters tape on a carpeted floor or rug and let your little one walk it like a balance beam or run cars over it like a track.

16. Gather some items on a table (not too small – choking hazards) and wrap masking tape (inside out) around your child's hand, and let them see what they can pick up on the tape. Sticky hands!

17. Make slime ahead of time. Your child will not want to stop playing with it. Better than Play-doh!

18. Give your child large (easy to remove) stickers to stick to a piece of paper or card stock. Super simple, clean, and fun. Kids love stickers.

19. Give your child pipe cleaners (chenille sticks) to poke through the holes in a plastic colander (pasta strainer).

A little bit of imagination and a few simple household staples is all that's needed to keep your little ones learning and smiling every day, while you and your older kids stay productive and on task.

If you'd like more suggestions for hands-on activities to do with your toddler or preschooler, feel free to check out my book *Little Sponges: Teaching Toddlers the Basic Concepts* on Amazon. This is my exact curriculum guide I used to teach all the children who came through my daycare program.

For those who are also using this time to potty train your little ones, I have a potty training guide that outlines all the tips and tricks I used to successfully train over fifty kids in my childcare career. You can find it on Amazon titled *Welcome to Poop Camp: The Truth, the Whole Truth, and Nothing but the Truth about Potty Training.*

Chapter 5

Break Before You Break Down

Being a stay-home or work-at-home mom is challenging enough. Add the element of having to not only become your child's teacher but do so during a world-wide quarantine, and you're bound to experience some stressful moments. It takes time to acclimate your family to the learning process. Give yourself some grace, and a BREAK!

At least once per hour, get up from your desk and move. Stretch your arms and legs, roll your neck, walk around a bit, even if it's a simple stroll to the mailbox or the path to the kitchen for a snack. Take a bathroom break. Not even kidding on this one! It's very easy to sit for hours without eating or stretching. Sometimes you even forget to empty your bladder.

Make sure you and your child take breaks. Schedule them or put on a timer if need be, to remind you both. Set it to your favorite song. The Qustodio app is very handy here because you are able to set time limits for your child's internet usage. If you set one hour at a time, you'll be able to stay on track with your work and be alerted when it's time to take a break. You can use this app on several devices and set rules per device. They send you a daily report as well, based on the parameters you set up. Granting or preventing access is immediate, which makes it very convenient if your child, say, runs out of time with their internet usage while doing an assignment, or you allow YouTube for a few minutes but then disable it again. It even has a free feature that allows you to see exactly what your child is searching for on Google or even texting to their friends. It might seem a bit invasive at first, but you'd be surprised by the level of temptation that arises in all ages of children when they have open access to the internet due to online schooling. It's so easy to open a new window when they think no one is looking. You can learn more about Qustodio by visiting https://www.qustodio.com/en/

In the beginning of this new arrangement where your child is home all day, it's going to feel as if he or she is eating everything in the home. This is just a phase. Your child is not used to having open access to food all hours of the day, so there is an adjustment period in play. The best way to handle this is to offer school-time approved snacks. In other words, snacks that can be consumed during school hours, preferably healthy ones rather than junk food.

Some examples would be fresh fruits and raw veggies, granola bars, popcorn, yogurt, rice cakes, almond butter, string cheese, and hard-boiled eggs. For little ones, you can create a daily snack pack. Once those snacks are gone, they can only have water or eat at the next meal. I also wouldn't recommend juice more than two times per day, and never (or at least, rarely) sodas. Junk food will make their bodies feel sluggish and cloud their focus. Sodas and sugary drinks can give them blood sugar spikes and offer a hard drop later in the day.

When you or your child is getting frustrated, it's a good idea to get up and walk away, even if it's not time for a break. For a few minutes, stretch, grab a snack, or even dance to your favorite song to get your blood pumping and release some energy.

Sitting at a computer for long periods of time is not only not good for our bodies, but it can also be damaging to our eyes. Staring at a screen for too long can cause tired eyes and headaches. Be sure to look away every few minutes. That's also one reason it's best for your child to take notes for classes in a physical notebook rather than in a Word program or on Notepad. Not everything needs to be digital. The screen time can be broken up a bit by doing this.

Don't be afraid to reach out to your child's teacher if you need help or don't understand something. That's their job. It's probably best to email first and call if you have an immediate need or don't hear back within 24 hours. It's easy to get behind or overwhelmed if too much time passes without turning in an assignment. Staying on task can help eliminate some stress.

I highly recommend shutting down laptops and devices when school work is over, not retreating to your rooms and watching TV or scrolling on your phones for the remainder of the day. Do something together that's not school or work related. Television is okay if it's a movie or a couple episodes of your favorite series, something measurable. Just be careful to not overdo the screen time. They've had plenty of that during the day. Be sure to add in some non-technical fun as well.

To recap, here are some things you can do to calm your mind and body to put yourself in an optimal state for productivity and success.

1. Yoga
2. Stretching or exercise
3. Dancing or singing to your favorite song
4. Journaling
5. Praying
6. Meditating
7. Having a conversation with a friend—uplifts your mood to stay connected
8. Focus on gratitude – maybe even get your kids to say what they're grateful for
9. Read something enjoyable or inspiring
10. Watch or listen to an inspiring or funny video or podcast

Just because school and work is important, it doesn't mean your day can't be fun. Find ways to incorporate music, movement, and laughter into your day to break up the monotony.

One more thing I'll share is to make sure that you, as the parent, walk away from the situation before it gets heated. Whether you're having a discussion about your teen going out of the house to see friends, a discussion with your spouse about the finances, or a school lesson you're working on with your younger child who is giving you attitude or "just isn't getting it," things can quickly escalate and cause you stress.

It's okay to take a few moments for yourself, breathe, assess your emotions, and come back to the situation with a new perspective. Staying in that moment, repeating the same things over and over, is not serving you or your child. It's like beating your head against a brick wall. Get outside or at least away from the desk for a few minutes and come back with a clear head. This goes for your work as well. Technical glitches and issues can become frustrating very quickly. Learn when to walk away.

Chapter 6

Mute out the Noise

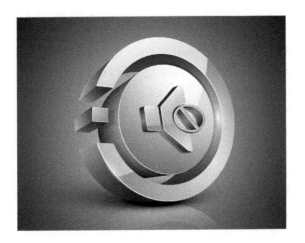

One thing to remember during this crisis, or really any time in life, is that the media is NOT our friend. It's there to sell stories, create a distraction from bigger issues, and rile people up, get them emotionally charged. Therefore, it's a good idea to make sure your child avoids media altogether, if possible, especially if they are young. Don't watch the news in front of your kids, if you must.

You can teach your teens to use discernment when reading, watching, or listening to the news. Teach them to go to direct sources for information rather than trusting what the media is trying to convey. Teach them to always check the source and compare data before sharing a picture or piece of content with their friends or even on social media.

Words *do* have power because of the emotions we attach to them. We must strive to protect our minds by filtering out the noise and negativity in the world. We must focus on the positive and the truth, and move toward solutions to keep from inciting fear in ourselves and others. Fear is nothing more than False Expectations Appearing Real, but what we focus on expands, so we must be careful.

Negativity doesn't just come from the media or strangers. It can come from our friends and family, and even our children. School can be stressful for kids, but it can be especially overwhelming when a child is thrown into a situation like the current quarantine we're facing, with little to no warning or preparation. Hurting people hurt people, so your child may lash out at you out of fear or anxiety or overwhelm. Don't take it personally. However, that kind of negative behavior and mindset isn't serving anyone in the situation, so be sure to nip it in the bud when it arises.

Social media can be a great way to stay connected to friends and family, but it can also be a command center for negativity, hatred, and uncensored comments. People become much braver when sitting behind a keyboard for some reason. Also stressful situations can bring out a very ugly side of people that we never expected. It's important to be aware, however, that people tend to show who they really are when faced with extreme situations. Kind, compassionate people tend to want to reach out and help others in whatever way they can. Self-centered, narcissistic people tend to lash out at others and look for people to blame for their pain. Again, teach your child that hurting people hurt people. Prepare them for the reality that people they know, or thought they knew, will surprise them by saying and doing things that seem out of character.

Since your child will also be online, interacting with peers and classmates, it's important to teach them that what they say to others through text can be misconstrued, so it's best to really consider what they want to say and how it will be perceived.

Another thing you'll want to keep in mind is that negativity can come from you as well, in the form of nagging, berating, and assessing your child constantly. It's best to focus on the effort rather than the result. For instance, if your child has a good attitude, is showing up for live lessons and taking notes but is holding steady Cs or Bs, it should be celebrated because they are giving their best effort. Grades are bound to suffer a bit during this time. Kids are stressed out by the new process and by not being able to see their teachers and friends every day. Many of their "constants" that brought them comfort in life, are gone. They may also be feeling the stress of parents who are now working from home or are out of work altogether. They could be picking up on the chaotic atmosphere or tension in the home or from their teachers until things get settled and all the kinks are worked out. Having a parent harp on them about not maintaining their normally high grades could just add to the problem. Encourage your child to do their best, and celebrate the effort, not just the result.

Some phrases that might help set an empowering tone are:

- Wow, you took some great notes today.
- You've really been working hard today.
- I'm proud of you for hanging in there and getting that portfolio done all on your own.
- I'm impressed by how you found the answers for yourself without having to ask the teacher or me.

- Wow, I wish I were as organized as you. That notebook looks great!

- I'm really proud of you for being prepared for class today. It makes the process flow much more smoothly.

- I really appreciate your great attitude today. I know math can be challenging for you sometimes.

Keep the tone in the home encouraging, educational, and light-hearted, and you will experience many less meltdowns in this process, from yourself and your child.

I'm going to switch gears and address one more issue that might be present right now: when a loved one is sick or has passed away due to this virus (or any other catastrophic situation you may be facing). This is real and should not be taken lightly. In many cases, people aren't even being able to hold a funeral or memorial service for their loved ones because of the quarantine. This is devastating for family members, and young children won't be able to understand it. Such a situation might even require professional help, such as a church counselor or family therapist to help people work through their emotions around such a devastating turn of events.

If you or your loved ones, especially your little ones, are having trouble dealing with an illness or death of a family member, I highly encourage you to speak to someone about it. It may help to simply talk to a friend or other family member, to reminisce about the good memories or sit and cry together. (the social distancing makes this even harder, I know)

Allow your children to ask questions, and answer them honestly without going into gory detail. Let them know they are encouraged to talk about it and ask questions as their feelings change or new information is presented. Pull together as a family and offer emotional support to one another. Teens may have a hard time expressing their emotions, so it's important to pay attention to their moods and signals that something may be bothering them. Don't hover, but be available to talk.

Offering books or movies that deal with this sort of crisis might be helpful right now. Of course, not ones that go into gory detail, but ones that offer practical, effective coping strategies or show people getting past the suffering and devastation, rebuilding their lives and moving forward. I'm not saying to use this as a bandage for the pain, more of a coping mechanism to accompany them in the grieving stage.

Chapter 7

Staying Connected with Friends and Family

One thing that helps kids and parents cope with home-schooling, online schooling, or simply working from home is staying connected with friends and family, especially in a quarantine situation. It's important to have real conversations with people, not just texting or messaging on social media; not just because text can be misconstrued, as I mentioned earlier in this book, but because there is something special about hearing people's voices and feeling their energy. We are all, after all, essentially balls of energy walking around on this earth, either attracting or repelling other balls of energy (other people).

It's one thing when you work or do school from home and you don't have time or the money to get out of the house on occasion, to get a change of scenery. It's a whole other feeling, such as being quarantined as we are currently, to not be *allowed* to leave your home. There's a sense of imprisonment and disconnect that can lead to anxiety, fear, and depression if not managed.

Here are a few ways to stay connected while also social distancing:

1. Get outdoors, with or without friends. Maintain the 6-foot distance rule if under quarantine. Getting fresh air and connecting with nature can be especially calming, refreshing, and reviving. As well, getting adequate sunshine can regulate melatonin in the body, which helps you sleep better; and vitamin D, which can protect against osteoporosis, cancer, depression, and muscle weakness.

2. Have regular video chats with your friends, family, teachers, and childcare providers. If your little ones normally attend daycare, it might help a lot to see and hear from their teacher/childcare provider. Perhaps the educator can read your child a bedtime story or do circle time with her class on a group Zoom. Get creative and don't be afraid to reach out. There's a good chance your child's teacher or childcare provider is missing your kids just as much.

3. You can also let a grandparent, aunt or uncle, or even older sibling read your child a bedtime story to stay connected.

4. Connect in Facebook groups. There is a group for pretty much any topic you can imagine these days – motorcycles, knitting, yoga, horses, dogs, art, and much more. Type a topic in the search bar and click on "groups" to find one you want to explore. Get in there and introduce yourself,

and start commenting on other people's posts to start conversations.

5. Pick up the phone and call a friend or loved one. People have more time than ever to have real conversations, and it's like a shot of dopamine when you hear a loved one's voice.

6. Write letters or have your kids write letters to friends or family members they miss. There is something special about receiving a hand-written correspondence, especially when it's so rare these days, world crisis or not. Text can also be effective on occasion, just to let someone know you're thinking about them.

7. Take this time to connect with the people in your home. Play board games, cook together, learn a new skill or hobby together, watch movies together, but be sure to have conversations while doing these things. The best time to learn more about your kids and teens is when you're having a conversation during normal activities.

8. Set up a virtual watch party with your friends, where you are all watching a TV show or movie together and commenting through text during it or setting up a Zoom or video chat discussion afterwards. Similar to a book club, but virtual.

9. Stream a DIY class to teach others something useful – cooking, sewing, mechanics, arts and crafts, digital design, home décor, or anything you are knowledgeable about. Many people are taking this time to learn new things. Be a leader!

10. Send quick video messages in Messenger if you don't want to do a full live chat.

Staying connected with your church family is another way to combat depression and loneliness. Most churches have livestream services set up these days so you can attend virtually. You could also set up a virtual Bible study group, a virtual Sunday School lesson, or a virtual prayer chat. You could even still use Zoom to practice songs with your choir group. Now is the time to get creative in communicating with other people. You could even start a prayer chat/chain in text if you want.

If you typically have a meet-up group of any kind, find a way to keep it going virtually: Mommy and Me, book clubs, wine clubs, game nights, pampering nights, Toastmasters classes, etc. All of these things can be held virtually if you get creative, or at least some variation of them.

Some people are close with their neighbors. Perhaps they hold a lot of movie nights, game nights, or barbecues, especially in warm weather. It's important to keep some of those traditions going and keep those relationships strong.

Some activities you could do within your neighborhood are:

- Take a walk with a neighbor and stay 6 feet apart
- Do yoga together but apart, in your backyards or on your front porches.
- Have the neighborhood kids play in the driveways and talk across the yard.
- Have a neighborhood chalk walk, where the kids go to different participating driveways and draw a picture with chalk.
- Have a dance party in your perspective driveways.
- Have a hula hoop contest or jump roping contest in your perspective driveways.
- Set up virtual play dates with little ones.

- Have a virtual trivia game night.
- Have a neighborhood parade with the little ones, making sure they stay far enough apart. You can use trikes, bikes, or simply walk with a windsock.
- Have a kite-flying party.

Some activities you could do with the people in your home to stay connected are:

- Pillow fights
- Movie nights
- Hide and seek
- Airsoft wars
- Corn hole
- Flag football
- Soccer
- Baseball
- Riding horses together – trail rides (if you have access to horses)
- Taking care of a farm
- Scavenger hunt / treasure hunt
- Trivia night
- Cooking party
- Cleaning party
- Hula hoop contest, jump rope contest
- Washing the cars together
- Gardening
- Kite flying

- Driveway art
- Walk your dog
- Create a vision board together
- Paint or do a craft
- Play with marbles
- Make leaf piles and jumping in them
- Build forts

The possibilities are endless if you use your imagination. When your kids look back on this crisis years from now, what will they remember most? Will they remember it as a time of fear, anxiety, and unease in the house? A time when Mom and Dad were on their phones constantly, and everyone in the household was off doing their own thing? Or will they remember it as a time of laughter, silliness, and togetherness? A time when the family was together more than usual, enjoying the outdoors or board games. You have the power to write the most amazing story your kids will ever remember, right now.

Chapter 8

Mind Your Marriage

It's also important to make time for your spouse during this situation. Your days may be even more stressful than usual, so make time for each other. You can make special dinners for one another, have a date night on the patio under the stars, or dance in your living room. One of my fondest memories from my childhood was seeing my daddy pull my mama out of the kitchen while she was cooking and bring her into the living room to dance with him. Us kids would sit and watch them dance and hold each other closely, and it made us feel safe and secure. Make time to hug and kiss your spouse in front of your children so they feel the love and security they need and deserve. Even something as simple as a drive around the block or a walk to the mailbox is quality time with your spouse if you allow it to be.

One of the biggest reasons couples divorce is disagreements when it comes to finances. Truly, it's typically not about the money at all but more about one partner growing and the other staying the same. Perhaps one partner wants to go back to school or wants to get out and socialize more. Maybe shopping has become therapeutic for one partner to fill a void. Partners might not see eye to eye on disciplining the children or what religion to raise them in.

Open, honest communication is the key to making a marriage work under any circumstances, but especially during a crisis when emotions are all over the map.

Here are a few ways couples can stay connected:

- Keep the lines of communication open. Share feelings of boredom, loneliness, resentment, and jealousy.

- Share ideas and dreams, no matter how far-fetched.

- Find at least one common interest, even better if it's a secret between the two of you – ballroom dancing, book club, wine club, etc.

- Don't resent your partner for not reading your mind. Be open and honest rather than offering passive-aggressive comments.

- Don't go outside your marriage to discuss problems or look for solutions, unless you do this together with a counselor or someone who is trained to deal with these situations.

- Allow one another solo activities on occasion. You don't have to do everything together. I can honestly say that my husband having a man cave made our marriage so much better.

- Maintain regular date nights – weekly, monthly

- Get away from the kids on occasion, even if it's to run to the grocery store, check the mail, or just go for a drive
- Be honest about the budget, spending habits, and income. Both partners need to be aware of the financial situation – assets, passwords, debt, etc. Secrets create separation.
- Set goals together – short term and long term
- Avoid the blame game. Mistakes and bad decisions happen. Deal with them together. Decide your options and create a plan to go from there.
- Practice gratitude and teach your kids to do the same.
- Deal with issues as they arise. Don't procrastinate or sweep things under the rug.
- Encourage one another rather than labeling or berating.
- Separate emotion and finances as much as possible, and don't let it carry over into the bedroom.

Our kids are always looking to us as parents to guide them and let them know they have a soft place to fall. This is going to be especially needed in a crisis situation, so it's important to make sure you are both on the same page and that you present a united front that provides a constant for your children, now and always.

Chapter 9

Protect Your Mental Capital

What are you doing to protect and strengthen your mind in this crisis? I already spoke about the negativity in the world and possibly in your home, but there is another aspect that needs to be addressed – your mental capital. Basically I mean what are you doing to grow during this time, to make sure you come out better and stronger on the other side of it?

We as humans aren't meant to merely survive in life, we're meant to thrive. We must do two things constantly in order to thrive: contribute and grow. When we're not doing these two things, we aren't living to our full potential. We aren't living fulfilled lives, and it's easy to fall into a depressed state, feel abandoned or isolated, especially during social distancing as we're experiencing right now. That simply adds fuel to the fire.

But how do we contribute when we're all practicing social distancing?

Here are a few ideas:

1. Offer to run errands (such as grocery shopping) for local neighbors or elderly people you know who can't get out and about. You don't have to come into contact with them. They can leave the money in an envelope on their porch, or they can send it to you through PayPal or Venmo. And you can leave the supplies on the porch when you return.

2. Use your skills/gifts to help others thrive in various areas of their lives: virtual teaching, virtual therapy or counseling, accounting services, virtual coaching, virtual fitness training, marketing tips/strategies for entrepreneurs, website design or other virtual business services, just to name a few.

3. Educate, inspire, and entertain others with your social media posts. Share DON'T scare! Keep it upbeat and helpful. Always ask yourself these three questions when you post something: Is this inspiring? Is this helpful? How am I making people feel with this post?

4. Pray for or with people you care about. Ask how this crisis is affecting them. Become a friend.

5. Share resources to help others find a job, save money, make money, save time, or solve a problem. Don't be a salesperson, be a friend.

6. Share supplies if you have extra.

7. Send care packages/meals to your neighbors, especially the elderly.

8. Do video chats to stay in touch with friends and family. Grandparents miss seeing their grandkids.

9. Donate food, cleaning supplies, gloves, masks, and toiletries to local shelters, nursing homes, or hospitals that are in need.

10. Tutor a student virtually.

Now that you know a few ways you can contribute, what can you do to strengthen your mental capital? (grow) It's all about self-care and giving back to others. We must recognize our self-worth and pour into ourselves before we're able to give anything to others. Otherwise, we will be attempting to give something we don't truly possess, which leaves us feeling depleted, tired, and overwhelmed. We can't pour from an empty cup. Therefore, we must be constantly pouring good things into our minds. Positivity. Gratitude. Hope. This is not the same as pretending everything in our lives is peachy. It's basically setting ourselves up to realize that even though there will be tough times, we won't crumble. We won't be defeated. We will make it through.

I highly encourage everyone to find two mentors. One should be what I call a distance mentor, someone who offers daily inspirational videos or podcasts that you can plug into to get new ideas and strengthen your faith and resolve. Some of my favorites are Tony Robbins, Dean Graziosi, Brené Brown, John Maxwell, Nick Santanastasso, Simon Sinek, Joel Osteen, Darren Hardy, and Trent Shelton. These are people you would most likely not be able to have on speed dial to call up when you're needing a pick-me-up, but you could watch one of their videos, read one of their books, or listen to one of their podcasts anytime you want.

The other type of mentor is what I call a close mentor. This is someone you could meet up with personally or at the least pick up the phone and call when you need to talk. This person should not be someone who will tell you what you need to hear. It needs to be someone who isn't afraid to kick your butt a little bit when you need it. But it needs to be someone you respect and will listen to, someone who has done or is doing something you want to accomplish, so they can guide you to reach your goals.

Both of these mentors are important, in my opinion, because one is a few steps ahead of you in life and the other is a few thousand steps ahead of you. The close mentor you can relate to on a more realistic level. The distance mentor is one you can aspire to become. After all, you should always have something to work toward.

The key is to fill your mind with educational and inspirational content to help you stay focused, productive, and moving forward in your life. If good content goes in, good results come out.

Here are 7 ways to keep your mind sharp and always be strengthening your mental capital:

1. Always be learning and creating new things
2. Use all 5 senses (or as many as possible) when learning something new. This helps you retain the information better and for longer.
3. Hold yourself to a higher standard. Write your own story. Don't blame memory problems on circumstances like your age or family history.
4. Use technology in an effective way – brain teasers, word games, trivia games, etc. to keep the mind sharp
5. Use multiple methods of receiving information: read it, write it, and say it

6. Don't cram information. Take breaks when needed, and take some time to absorb what you've read or learned so far. Don't fly through a book or training. Speed reading is fine as long as you actually understand what you've read.

7. Use mnemonic devices to remember things: for example RICE – rest, ice, compression, elevation (this is a mnemonic device that doctors and medical professionals use for treating injuries and inflammation)

Another thing you can do to strengthen your mental capital during this time is to create something. Write a book, create a podcast or a course, create a mastermind (Facebook) group, create a book club or wine club, or create a support group for moms. Now is the perfect time to dig deep and either discover or hone some of your other amazing skills, and find ways to use them to offer value to others. If you're a chef, create a simple, budget-friendly meal planner. If you're a musician or artist who can't book gigs right now, create a course or offer personal music lessons virtually. If you're an administrative assistant who can't go into the office or has been laid off, create a course or write a book about how to manage an office efficiently, how to organize your office, or simple tricks for using Quick Books. There are so many ways you can use your other talents to offer value and help others through a crisis like this. It's all about who you want to become in this process and how you will *grow* through it, not just go through it.

One more effective way to contribute and grow every single day is to ask yourself: who can I help, and how can I help them? When you focus on that, you will always be moving the needle forward in your life, which results in more fulfillment and joy and prevents depression.

Here is a list of 10 books that I highly recommend to strengthen your mental capital:

Think and Grow Rich – Napoleon Hill

Rich Dad, Poor Dad – Robert Kiyosaki

Unshakeable – Tony Robbins

Dare to Lead – Brené Brown

15 Invaluable Laws of Growth – John Maxwell

Girl, Wash Your Face – Rachel Hollis

The Underdog Advantage: Rewrite Your Future By Turning Your Disadvantages Into Your Superpowers – Dean Graziosi

Get Out Of Your Head: Stopping the Spiral of Toxic Thoughts – Jennie Allen

The One Thing: The Surprisingly Simple Truth Behind Extraordinary Results – Gary Keller

Chapter 10

Dealing with Your Quaran-teen

Relating to and parenting teens during a quarantine is definitely not the same as dealing with younger kids, especially if your teen is of driving age and a social butterfly. They are going to resist the rules and campaign to hang out with their friends despite the dangers. This is particularly true if your child is typically in public school and they're now "stuck at home" with no one to talk to or hang out with except their immediate family.

As well, teens have more access to social media and the regular media, so they are probably hearing lots of stories from their friends and reading numerous headlines. Their heads may be spinning from trying to process all that information. They may be feeling scared, worried, angry, or nervous about what's going on, and they are looking to the adults in their lives to make sense of everything, to keep them as close to their "normal" life as possible in this situation.

How does a parent handle the questions, the arguments, the anger, and all the other emotions that come along with a crisis like this?

There are no easy answers, but here are a few ways you can support your teen during a crisis (specifically a quarantine):

1. Manage your own anxiety first. Only rely on facts, straight from the source. Take care of your mental and physical health to stay on top of things. Share your concerns in an educational and empowering way with your teen. Try to focus on sharing the positive and encouraging headlines rather than the death tolls and negative comments from the media.

2. Ask your teen what they know about what's going on. Ask what their concerns are. Ask how THEY think the situation should be handled, what they would do if they were in power. Ask them how they're feeling.

3. Validate their feelings and concerns. Reassure them by sharing the steps you're taking toward protecting them and the entire family, and why you're taking these steps.

4. Be available for new questions based on updates. Let them know they can come to you with new questions or concerns. Have regular check-ins to see how they're feeling about the situation. Ask them to repeat their understanding of what's going on, back to you.

5. Empower them through the behavior you model concerning hygiene (for the virus) and precautions you're taking. Praise them when they make good/safe choices.

6. Reassure them that your family will make it through this together by reminding them of situations you've overcome as a family in the past – perhaps a family death, a house fire, or any other crisis-themed event.

7. Don't blame others and feed into the negativity. Don't tell your teen about every statistic you read or hear. It only incites fear and uncertainty.

8. Offer video chats with their friends.

9. Offer supervised hangouts – where you or another adult ensures the 6-foot rule.

10. Offer virtual movie nights – already mentioned in a previous chapter.

11. Plan some fun things to do for when the crisis is over. Give them something to look forward to and remind them that this will not last forever.

12. No sleepovers or touching – hand shakes, hugs, fist bumps, etc. (during a virus quarantine) Remember, anyone can be an asymptomatic carrier.

If your teen has a boyfriend or girlfriend, and you're going through a crisis that involves limiting human contact – such as the virus we're facing—you cannot allow them to be together unsupervised. As hard as it will be, you must remain firm with your house rules of no contact other than virtual. Like I mentioned, as of the time of writing this book, our world has suffered over 100,000 deaths from this virus, and we are under a strict quarantine. Extreme measures are in place to keep our loved ones safe. You may not be going through this exact type of crisis, but a lot of the tips shared in this chapter will be helpful in any tough situation.

One way to keep your teen from being upset about the "lockdown" is to make sure you spend some family time together. Refer back to the activities in Chapter 7 of this book for ideas. Also, don't try to use this time to get your teen to "look on the bright side" of things. It's just not going to happen. Instead, don't be afraid to say, "This sucks and I'm sorry you're dealing with something like this right now, but it won't last forever. What can I do to make it easier on you, that doesn't put our family at risk?"

You could even drive your teen over to see their boyfriend or girlfriend, and make sure they stay 6 feet apart when hanging out. Make it brief, just enough to allow them some time together. It's going to be challenging, but at least you can let your teen know you're doing your best with the hand you've been dealt. Let them know you care about their feelings.

Don't allow your teen to stay on the phone (or laptop) or on social media all day. Make sure they get some family time and non-tech time. Also, make sure they don't stay holed up in their room all day without socializing with the family. Human connection is vital during a situation like this, and since they can't get it from their typical social group, it must come from their immediate family. Make sure you're not neglecting your teen by focusing too much on work or your own social activities.

With teens you must stay firm while also letting them know you sympathize with them and value their input. That doesn't mean you will let them make their own rules. It simply means you will hear them out. They just want to be heard and know that their opinions and feelings matter.

Chapter 11

Food Staples that Will Sustain Your Family

'm sure many of you have already felt the dent in your wallet from your food budget increasing by having your kids home all day right now. I mentioned in Chapter 5 about creating snack packs for younger kids, but teens are a whole different situation. Most of them will eat twice as much during the day and snack on anything that draws their interest, usually junk food if it's in the house. The best way to prevent this, of course, is to not have those things in the house. But, if you can't avoid that, then I would make a rule that only allows a certain amount of these foods per day.

For instance, no more than 1 soda per day (which is still bad for them), chips only with sandwiches at meals, water in between meals, eat at least 2 fruits or vegetables every day(should be more), just to name a few. Ramen noodles is another favorite of teens. They will eat their weight in those things if they can. But those are loaded with sodium, so it's best to limit those as well. There is only so much you can do to prevent teens from eating poorly, so I'll leave the rest of that to your discretion.

With that said, having all your kids at home all day and cooking three meals per day, (especially when restaurants are closed for quarantine, like what we're dealing with), we have to get creative as parents. There are some staple items that can save you money and feed a large family on a tight budget. Keep in mind, not all of these are super healthy, but you can look for gluten-free or healthy versions of these in your local stores.

Here are 17 staples to help you save money on your grocery bill and feed a large family:

1. Pasta – spaghetti noodles, tri-colored pasta (pasta salad), angel hair pasta, macaroni, etc. The possibilities are almost endless for pasta.

2. Rice – again, many options here. You can buy big bags of white or brown rice and add your own seasonings, or you can get the Ready Rice (which I prefer) that is already flavored and offers many options.

3. Beans – can substitute for meat in tacos, burgers, and soups.

4. Bread – sandwich bread, hamburger buns, hot dog buns, French bread, etc. Or you can buy flour, shortening, and milk to make your own.

5. Go-to seasonings. This is going to be your saving grace with many meals. If you can make it taste good enough, you can substitute a lot of sides or veggies for expensive meats. I like Mrs. Dash and Pink Himalayan salt personally.

6. Tortillas – so many possibilities here. You can make quesadillas, wraps, burritos, tacos, and more. Simply add a few pieces of chicken or beef, maybe some black beans and rice, and top off with some tomatoes and lettuce, and you've got a quick, easy, filling meal.

7. Tomato-based sauces – spaghetti, pizza, sloppy joes, etc. Throw some ground beef or ground turkey in there, and you can end up with a big meal that goes a long way.

8. Potatoes – baked, hash browns, mashed, scalloped, etc.

9. Eggs – use for cooking and baking, add to rice for fried rice, hard boil them to serve as a meat substitute, cook them many different ways for breakfast.

10. Frozen veggies – soups, pot pies, casseroles. Or you can get raw veggies and enjoy as snacks.

11. Flour – self-rising for biscuits, gravy, thicken soups, make homemade dough for all sorts of dishes.

12. Peanut butter – use to make sandwiches, dips, energy bites, spread on rice cakes, cookies, etc.

13. Chicken and beef stock or bouillon cubes

14. Cream of chicken and cream of mushroom soups – good for casseroles, Salisbury steak, chicken and dumplings, pot pies, etc.

15. Shredded and sliced cheese – use on sandwiches, burgers, fries, baked potatoes, in casseroles, pastas, rice, and more.

16. Boneless chicken, ground beef, ground turkey – great staple meats to keep around. Buy in bulk and portion into Ziploc bags for several meals.

17. Cereal and milk – I'll let you use your discretion as to what types of cereals to buy, but just know that most teens don't eat the nice, healthy versions of cereal. Also, they eat A LOT of cereal, so expect a good portion of your budget to go to cereal and milk. Just saying. Cereal is considered pretty much one of the main food groups as far as teens are concerned.

One thing you can do is go grocery shopping with a friend and divide the meats/frozen veggies between your two households, to save on cost and get great deals on bulk foods you both use.

You can also cut coupons to save money. Although, I will say, in my experience, I never saved much from couponing because the majority of the items that offered coupons was junk food, not fresh meats or dairy or produce. It can save you on nonfood items sometimes. You just have to become very savvy at using them. It was too much of a learning curve for me.

Here are a few other tips to help you save money on food, by preserving the food to last longer:

- Bananas: separate the bunch so that none of them are touching one another

- Strawberries – turn the container upside down in the fridge and don't wash them all at once. Wash one at a time as you eat them.

- Don't store apples and oranges together. They will ripen much more quickly. But apples and potatoes work well together.

- Ripen an avocado by placing it in a brown paper bag on the counter. Once cut open, either eat the entire avocado in one sitting or wrap the remaining portion tightly in plastic wrap and eat it within the next 24 hours.

- Evenly place items in the fridge and don't overfill the shelves. It prevents proper air flow.

- Don't wash produce before storing it in the fridge. The moisture encourages mold growth.

- Store frequently used items at the front of the fridge, so they are easily accessible, and energy and coolness is not wasted with the fridge door open to search for items.

One quick tip I'll leave you with, that works more on little kids than older ones, involves dealing with "the hangries" as I call them. The moments when your kids come tell you they're so hungry, but it hasn't been long since their last meal, and they've already had a snack. They may not be hungry but thirsty instead. Therefore, tell your child to go drink 8 ounces of water and wait thirty minutes. If they are still "hungry" after doing that, then they can have a piece of fresh fruit or veggie to tie them over until the next meal. That will at least buy you some time and make sure they are getting proper hydration as well. I call that a mom win.

Chapter 12

Making Money in Spite of the Madness

his chapter is going to dive a bit deeper to offer some ways of making money from home when you've been laid off during a crisis related to a pandemic like the one we're dealing with now, but I'm also going to offer some options that would be viable during a normally functioning economy. You can tweak these as needed, but hopefully these ideas will get your wheels turning and spring you into action.

First, here are 7 ways to make money on the side, that do not conflict with your current business, whatever that may be:

- Create content for entrepreneurs – blogs, Facebook pages, websites, Facebook ads or other ad campaigns, if you're great with writing.
- Create/edit photos for marketing purposes
- Edit content for authors and other professionals – books, ad copy, blog content, book blurbs, etc.
- Teach something – develop a course on social media marketing, general marketing, financial strategies, mindset strategies, Facebook lives, etc.
- Offer virtual services for other entrepreneurs – become a virtual assistant, offer web design or building sales funnels
- Offer home cleaning/organizational services for busy moms or entrepreneurs
- Offer consulting services such as business coaching, life coaching, strategies for time management and marketing

Notice one of the big trends in this list is marketing. That's because anyone who has a business, online or offline, will always need to learn about marketing. It's the lifeblood of their success, and I encourage all business owners to learn at least the basics.

The top 5 fields that will never become obsolete and that typically yield high income opportunities are copy writing, consulting, internet marketing, speaking, platform selling – courses – and investing. Choose one of these categories and get going!

Before this pandemic hit, there were certain businesses that were on the "no worries" list, meaning these businesses would thrive no matter what happened in the economy. Everything changed with this virus.

The industries that were on this list, as of just three months before this virus hit were:

- Food and beverage industry – most restaurants and bars have been shut down indefinitely or have transitioned to drive-through or pick up only, and have lost lots of revenue.

- Retail consignment – all consignment shops are closed indefinitely, and most retail stores have limited hours now.

- Information technology – building websites, teaching marketing strategies or offering courses – these will always thrive.

- Repair industry – auto mechanics, woodworking, etc. These have either shut down or are limited in their customer base.

- Health care – this one will always be in demand because people are always dying and others being born.

- Cleaning services – most residential businesses are completely shut down right now because people won't allow others into their homes. Commercial cleaning businesses are still somewhat thriving because these services can be completed after hours.

- Real estate and investments – typically this would be an ideal way to make money, but as most of us may remember the crash of 2007/2008, things can change drastically and quickly. As well, many real estate investors and banks have lost a ton of money with this particular crisis we're in because tenants and homeowners can't afford their rent and mortgages due to being laid off.

As soon as the virus hit, the list changed to these Recession-Resistant Industries:

- Grocery stores and Discount retailers – Dollar General and the Dollar Tree stores have been booming! Grocery stores can barely keep food and supplies on the shelves.

- Alcoholic Beverage Manufacturing and Sales – I never knew until the past month just how essential an alcoholic beverage store actually was. Come to find out it's because of several reasons: 1. Alcoholics could go into severe detox and flood the hospitals or even die. 2. Alcoholic beverage sales and taxes are a huge part of the economy. 3. Alcoholic beverage stores sell water and other drinks.

- Cosmetics – two things women will not give up, even in a crisis – typically, are mascara and foundation. However, they will switch to a more sensibly priced brand if need be, so the pricing must be competitive. Salon hair products and services tend to be the last luxury service to go.

- Death and funeral services – as I mentioned, people are always being born as others are dying.

- Consumer Goods / Staples – as we are experiencing with the whole toilet paper pandemic. However, other staples such as hand soap, hand sanitizer, and cleaning products are in short supply as well. There are just so many little things that we as a society took for granted without realizing it. Now we're being forced to pay attention.

- Doctors and medical workers – these will always be in demand because people will always get sick, have babies, and need emergency services.

Now that you know what the most in-demand, non-commodity industries are, you may be thinking of some new careers or entrepreneurial ventures to explore. I encourage you to choose a few, look at the pros and cons of each, and ask yourself what's the ONE thing you'd be excited to get up and do every single day if money were no factor. Then find a career or business venture that aligns with that activity and go for it!

Before I close this chapter on money-making , I want to leave you with a few tips on mindset around money. There are some ingrained beliefs that you've likely picked up in your life that may be holding you back from wealth. I want to take a moment to explore and address these so you're aware of them and can overcome them when they arise.

1. Negative associations with money and wealth. Here are a few phrases closely associated with this belief that you've likely heard and now believe somewhere deep inside you:
   - money doesn't grow on trees
   - money is the root of all evil
   - money can't buy happiness
   - money will make you a bad person/greedy
   - rich people are greedy
   - truly helping someone doesn't involve you asking them for money – it should be free

   Now I want to offer some phrases to combat and overcome those negative thought processes:

   - the more money I make, the more I can help others – money offers options
   - you should love what you do so much that the only way you can make money from it is by helping others

- typically, people who say negative things about money have money problems and they are speaking out of pain or scarcity mindset
- I deserve wealth and abundance because I am meant for great things and meant to help a lot of people
- people need me to keep going and be successful so I can offer hope and solutions to their problems

2. You're overly sensitive to other people's opinions, perceptions, and criticisms.

- you try to make sure everyone likes you
- you try not to offend anyone
- you try to not bring attention to yourself

3. You fear change or aren't willing to pay the high cost of success, so you come up with excuses such as:

- maybe I'm just not good enough
- maybe I don't have what it takes
- maybe I'm not meant to have more success than this – this is as far as I'm meant to go
- I'm not worthy of wealth
- other people deserve success more than me

You must get comfortable with being a little bit uncomfortable for a while. Acquiring success means you'll be required to change and grow along the way. We don't go into business, we *grow* into leadership.

4. Realizing you're unwilling to pay the price but equally unwilling to admit it. Pride! Blame! Denial!

- that life is just not for me
- I'm just "not that kind of person" – I'm not "a salesperson"

- I don't need money or success to be happy

Let me just take a moment here to mention that being humble doesn't mean you don't deserve wealth. Wealth and fame only enhance who we really are deep down inside, so if you're worried you'll become someone else, just know that you'll only become an enhanced version of who you truly are. If you're a good person who cares about helping others, you'll be able to reach and help even more people when you grow your wealth and resources.

Success has a price that you pay in advance, and the cost is higher than you think. It can cause you to lose friends (just know that a true friend is happy for you even when they aren't happy for themselves), lose connections in social groups, and lose comfort within yourself and perhaps feel a bit awkward around others if they start treating you differently. My suggestion is to find friends who don't just celebrate you and cheer you on when *they* are winning in life.

Now that you have learned about money beliefs and a few ways to create more income, here are a few immediate steps you can take to enhance your finances immediately in an economic crisis:

- Pay down debt, especially high-interest debt such as credit cards. If the government is offering small business or personal loans with low or no interest, such as they are right now, take advantage of that to consolidate all your credit cards and loans to one account. Peace of mind is priceless.

- Boost your emergency savings. Take your entertainment funds and put them into savings right away. Look for free/low-cost entertainment options for a while to continue saving money. Focus on saving $100, then $200, then $500, and keep going.

- Identify ways to cut back in expenses – cable, Amazon Prime, subscriptions for non-essential items, gym memberships, etc.

- Live within or below your means for a while. Put the majority of your income toward necessities only.

- Focus on the big picture rather than instant gratification. Make sure to have some cash on hand or stashed away somewhere, but work toward a few long-term investments as well.

- Build relationships for your business NOW. Connect with new people and reconnect with old friends. You never know how you might be able to bring value to one another down the road. Perhaps you can help someone find a job, a new side income, a new doctor or mechanic. Nothing will ever replace the value of word-of-mouth referrals. Keep in mind that now is a crucial time to take care of your current customers. Send hand-written notes or texts, offer free gifts or coupons for loyalty or for referring someone to you, call to see how they are fairing in this situation – ask if they need anything. Let them know you are a human first and a business person second.

- Build up your skills. Learn new online platforms, learn or hone marketing/sales skills, learn a new craft or build onto an existing one.

- Create a side income. I will always recommend having more than one stream of income, just as the financial geniuses of the world do. In fact, most of them recommend five or more streams. I would highly encourage you to create at least two. You'll realize the power of this when an economic crisis hits, believe me.

I would like to share one more powerful thought with you, about residual income. This is a word that I'm sure you've heard many times, especially recently with so many people promoting their "side hustle from home" opportunities. However, it's important to know the difference between renewed income and residual income.

Renewed income is money that you must show up every day, week, month, and year to renew or reactivate. In other words, if you don't do the work, you don't get paid. This type of income is most prevalent in traditional jobs. You show up, work the hours expected, and you collect your paycheck at the end of the week. The problem with this is once you cash that paycheck, you've just cancelled all the work you did that week. You must now start over and do the process again.

Now, please understand that I'm not bashing or condemning that type of work situation. I did it for many years. It provides a sense of structure and security that is very attractive and comforting for most people. I'm not here to encourage you to quit your day job if it's putting food on the table for your family. I'm simply encouraging you to also explore a side income to start building residual income. This is money that shows up repeatedly even if you don't. You create it one time and it pays you over and over.

Here is a simple but powerful example of residual income:

$100 per month – coming in every month for work you did one time – is equivalent to having $24,000 in the bank earning 5% interest

$200 per month is like having $48,000 in the bank earning 5% interest

$500 per month is like having $120,000 in the bank earning 5% interest

$5000 per month is like having $1,200,000 in the bank earning 5% interest

So that means, even if you start building something that is earning you a mere $100 per month on top of your regular job, that is an extra $1200 in your pocket every year. Can you think of some bills that could help pay? Some stress that would help alleviate in your family?

One of my gifts is helping others discover their unique gifts and helping them find ways to monetize those gifts. I have a side business that truly fulfills me and pays me well for work I do one time, even in a crisis situation like what we're experiencing now, but I know that not everyone is meant to do what I do. Plus, I don't want people joining my business who don't see the vision that I see in what I do.

However, if you are open to new sources of income, I'm happy to have a chat and discuss some options with you. I can be reached at tsanderspublishing@yahoo.com or you can connect with me through Facebook (traci.sanders.399).

As well, if you're an entrepreneur who is looking for social media marketing tips or strategies for your business, feel free to request to join my private Facebook group where I go LIVE three days a week speaking on these very topics, as well as touching on mindset. It's called Social Savvy Sisters in Success. You must answer a few questions to be accepted into the group. There is no soliciting or poaching in this group, and it's not focused on engagement. It's more of a library/resource for those who need ongoing strategies for their businesses. It's for women only, and we all behave like ladies in there. Be sure to read the description before requesting to join. Hope to see you in there!

I'll leave you with 10 phrases (affirmations) that can attract more money into your life. You're welcome to discount them if you want, but these have been powerfully effective in my life for years.

- I am a money magnet. I attract wealth and prosperity in everything I do.
- There's plenty more where that came from. (I say this one when I pay my bills or tithes)
- Money flows freely and abundantly to me.
- My income exceeds my expenses every month. (rather than saying: we never have enough money)
- My income is constantly growing.
- I choose to live a rich, full life.
- I give myself permission to prosper and grow.
- I deserve to be paid well for my gifts and skills.
- I am wealthy in all areas of my life.
- I attract the people and circumstances into my life that allow me to live abundantly.

Chapter 13

Healthy Habits to Protect Your Family

ecause the crisis we happen to be dealing with involves
our health, I thought it would not only be appropriate but
also important to include a chapter about protecting and
maintaining our health.

Stress is one of the worst things for our bodies, and any world
crisis is going to perpetuate some stress, which can manifest in
the body in different ways. It can cause body aches, inflammation,
headaches, illness, and more.

I've already given you some tips on strengthening your mental
capital and keeping your mind sharp, so I'll focus on the physical
body for a moment.

As I've mentioned, it's important to move your body every day, to keep your muscles and joints fluid and flexible. However, after sitting at a desk for hours, our bodies can develop cramps and pains that need to be alleviated immediately. Stretching and targeting pressure points in the body can help.

Here are 5 pressure points in the body that instantly relieve stress:

- Hands – wrap your hands in a warm, moist towel for a few minutes then gently take the thumb and middle finger of your left hand (thumb on top and middle finger underneath) and press in between the thumb and pointer finger of the other hand, in that dip. Breathe in and out slowly for 15 seconds, focusing on your breath and releasing stress and tension. Switch and do the same with the other hand.

- Wrists – with your thumb and middle finger of the left hand (thumb on top and middle finger underneath, press gently in the center just below your right wrist, while curling your hand toward you as you breathe in and extending it back outward as you release that breath. Do this for 15 seconds and then switch to the other hand.

- Third eye – using your ring and middle finger, find the spot between your eye brows and gently press. Breathe deeply in and out for 15 seconds as you apply the pressure.

- Elbow – this pressure point can relieve all sorts of issues such as anxiety or nervousness, and it can even help with digestive issues that are related to these feelings. Open your right arm outward and using your thumb on top and middle finger underneath find the divot in the crook of your elbow. Press gently on this dip and breathe in and out for 15 seconds.

- Feet – press on the high point of your big toe with your thumb on top and your middle and ring finger underneath, right on the knuckle area. You can also do this by applying pressure to the area where the ball of the foot and the ankle meet. Breathe in and out slowly for 15 seconds. Doing this has been known to reduce stress and lower blood pressure.

As you do any of these exercises, be sure to focus on your breath and visualize the stress as a physical ball of energy that you are releasing into the universe and out of your body. It works!

Now that you have a few strategies to immediately reduce stress and anxiety, lets tackle some other things that could be contributing to other health issues you may be experiencing – skin irritations (eczema), allergies, respiratory issues (which is definitely applicable to the virus crisis we're dealing with right now), and overall health.

Did you know there are a few everyday items in your home that could be deteriorating your health, zapping your energy, attacking your lungs, and damaging your skin? This is where I'm most knowledgeable and can help others. It's what I do for a living. I help families convert their homes to affordable, nontoxic cleaning and personal care options to improve their overall health.

Here are a few simple switches you can make in your home for better health:

1. Laundry detergent – this is the #1 culprit in your home for allergies, eczema, and even contributes to autoimmune diseases. It makes sense because we wash our bed covers and pillow cases in laundry detergent, then we breathe in those chemicals during the night. We wash our clothes with laundry detergent, then they rub against our skin all

day and night. Making this ONE switch will offer you huge improvement in your health very quickly!

2. Hand soap – most hand soaps on the market contain irritants and chemicals such as triclosan and parabens that strip your skin of nutrients and cells that keep your skin healthy and supple. Think about how many times you have to put lotion on after washing your hands, or at night when they've been dried out from the weather or repeated hand washing, especially during a wide-spread pandemic related to a virus. But this truly applies to everyday normal life as well. Find a soap that doesn't contain these chemicals and your skin will thank you! The same goes for shampoos and body lotions as well.

3. All purpose cleaners and disinfectants – a study was released in 2018 called the Lung Damage Study where over 6000 participants (men and women) were asked to clean their homes just one time per week using the major store brands most people have in their homes – Gain, Tide, Lysol, Scrubbing Bubbles, etc. What they found was at the end of the 20-year study, there was as much damage to the participants' lungs as if they'd smoked a pack of cigarettes per day for those 20 years. That's mind blowing, but it makes sense when you think about the horrible smells you detect even when you're aisles away from the cleaning section of the grocery store. The big manufacturers have to use chemical fillers and water to be able to cut manufacturing costs and pay their overhead. But just think about what these products are doing to our health – getting into our food from our dishes, getting on our skin, and getting into our lungs.

I highly encourage you to find some nontoxic cleaners to replace these with. I know some of you probably use vinegar and baking soda, and if that works for you then stick with that. I personally detest the smell of vinegar, so I found a better option that works for my family.

The products I represent are plant-based, have no childproof caps, and are concentrated – no water or fillers – to save you money. In fact, the online store where I get these products, that I've been shopping at for years and have converted everything in my home, has hundreds of safer, healthier products for the home. Feel free to reach out to me at tsanderspublishing@yahoo.com or connect with me on Facebook (traci.sanders.399) to learn more. I'm happy to give you a tour of the store to see if there are some items you could switch out in your home that fit your family's budget.

In the meantime, here are a few other simple things you can do to help boost your health:

- Take vitamin C and an immune complex every day
- Take a highly-absorbed multivitamin every day
- Drink plenty of water to flush out toxins
- Stretch and exercise your body every day
- Eat breakfast (preferably with protein) every day
- Limit your sugar intake
- Limit your processed foods intake
- Eat lots of green, leafy veggies to help scrub your insides (gut) and flush out toxins
- Drink lemon water to help flush out toxins
- Observe portion control in your meals – eat 5 times per day rather than 3 big meals

- Take a high quality probiotic every day – yogurt is not enough
- Take zinc every day
- Add green plants to your home to help remove toxins in the air
- Avoid chemical-filled candles, wax melts, and plug-in air fresheners
- Limit refined carbohydrates – white bread and potatoes
- Avoid fried foods
- Avoid sodas and sugary beverages
- Limit red meat – burgers and steaks
- Avoid margarine
- Buy well-made shoes – protects from join pain, back pain, and knee pain
- Track your movement on a phone app or wrist watch
- Get adequate sleep – 7-9 hours nightly

As a bonus, here are 10 foods that fight inflammation and joint pain to keep your body moving freely:

1. Tomatoes
2. Extra-virgin olive oil
3. Green, leafy veggies
4. Nuts – almonds, pecans, walnuts
5. Fatty fish – salmon, mackerel, sardines
6. Fruits – berries, cherries, oranges
7. Avocados
8. Bell peppers and chili peppers

9. Mushrooms

10. Dark chocolate

Again, many people are sitting on the couch or at a desk for hours in a day now, whereas they used to go to the gym, go for a walk with friends, or at least walk around their offices. Therefore, it's more important now than ever before to make sure we give our bodies the proper nutrition and supplements, keep moving, and watch what we put in and on our bodies through daily use products. All of these steps combined will put your body in a peak state of performance and offer sustained energy that makes you feel unstoppable in your day!

Chapter 14

Controlling the Chaos and Clutter

One thing I'm hearing a lot of moms say is that their homes are a daily, endless battle. I can relate to your pain.

I heard a saying once that goes: trying to clean the house while the kids are home is like trying to shovel snow during a snowstorm. It's a futile effort.

Again, I've been there. With 4-6 daycare kids and my own three home every day, I constantly dealt with chaos and clutter. The first thing I found that helped was to establish a routine for the little ones. There were certain times of the day that we designated for "clean up," usually before we transitioned into another activity such as lunch or playground time. It was scheduled and predictable, and even though the kids didn't know how to read a clock, they knew the "season" of what was expected during the day.

I involved them in the clean-up process by creating designated piles of toys and items that each one was responsible for putting away before they could join us in the next activity. This not only taught responsibility but it also reinforced the concept of knowing where those items belonged in the play area.

Another thing you can do is offer a little friendly competition. Play a song that the kids know very well, and see if they can get their "mess" cleaned up before the song ends. ("Beat the song") Kids really enjoy this activity.

Make sure you have organized the home in a way that your kids (of all ages) know where to put things away. For instance, when your older kids unload the dishwasher, do they know where the dishes go, or do you move things around constantly? Don't go behind them and "reorganize" the dishes in the dishwasher, unless you're teaching them a more efficient way, not just your control-freak method. (yep, I'm guilty of that one) Let them do it their way and see if the dishes get cleaned. My philosophy is, as long as we both get the desired result, the process doesn't matter. (hello, New Math?)

Here are some other hacks to speed your daily house cleaning and keep things tidy:

- Clean as you go throughout the day. Make sure the dishwasher is emptied every morning and is ready for dirty dishes to be loaded as you go through them in the day. This makes a huge difference. That way, all the dishes are loaded by the end of dinner and the dishwasher is ready to be started.

- Dust your baseboards with dryer sheets. Even the little kids can do this one. Bonus, it will make your house smell amazing.

- Clean a room top to bottom and left to right. That way you're not constantly going back over an area. Vacuum last, after dusting the ceiling fans and blinds, for example.

- Keep extra plastic bags in the bottom of the trash cans. That way, when one is removed, a new one is ready to be installed.

- Create a cleaning caddy/shelf for each bathroom, with its own supplies, including gloves and scrubbers if necessary. That way, your kids can't use the excuse of "I can't find the cleaning stuff" or "I'll wait until you're done with the gloves" to get started.

- Clean in categories: trash first, clothes/shoes, then papers and books. That's pretty much all that should be in a room anyway. It breaks the job up into small, manageable steps.

- Put tennis balls in your dryer to fluff up comforters and blankets.

- Add an extension cord to your vacuum cleaner to avoid wasting time re-plugging it in as you clean.

- Listen to upbeat music as you clean, not slow tunes. Keeps you moving faster.

- Have a mail bin to organize your mail as it comes in, right by the door if possible.

- Have a hamper in the bedroom closet and the bathroom – one for wet items and one for dry ones.

- Choose one room per day to tidy, usually the main area of the house – living room and kitchen.

- Have a collection bin in the corner of the living room or den (main area of activity) where you place items you collect throughout the day. Have your children / family come collect their belongings from that central basket at the end of each day. That puts the responsibility back on them and keeps your main living area clutter free.

- Involve the kids in the cleaning – make it a game, as I mentioned above. You can even say something like: the first one to clean up their pile properly gets to choose dinner or the family movie tonight.

There's also something I call the Ten-Minute Tidy where at the end of the day, or a few times during the day, you set a timer for 10 minutes and the family does as much cleaning as they can during that span of time. It's amazing how much can truly get done when a timer and deadline is involved.

Keeping a clean home begins with what you bring into the home. Therefore, it's a good practice to take something out as you bring something in. However, some of us have already accumulated a number of items that we need to now sift through. Now is a good time to de-clutter your home.

Here is a list of 50 things you can throw away to declutter your home. You can choose one per day if you want.

1. Old couch pillows
2. Old magazines
3. Movies you don't watch
4. Movies that are scratched
5. Burned-out candles
6. Extra cords
7. Games with missing pieces

8. Old books
9. Broken cosmetics
10. Old nail polish
11. Old perfume
12. Old toothbrushes
13. Half-empty bottles
14. Towels with holes
15. Anything you haven't used in the last month
16. Socks without matches
17. Socks with holes
18. Underwear with holes
19. Clothes you haven't worn in 6 months
20. Clothes that don't fit
21. Earrings without a match
22. Old ties
23. Old belts
24. Old purses
25. Old hats and gloves
26. Worn-out shoes
27. Worn-out blankets
28. Old pillows and sheets
29. Expired food
30. Take-out menus
31. Restaurant sauce packets
32. Old coupons
33. Old cleaning supplies

34. Anything you have too much of
35. Cups with missing pieces – coffee cups
36. Rags with holes
37. Excess Tupperware and bowls without matching lids
38. Old mail
39. Expired medication
40. Old manuals – you can find them online now
41. Old receipts
42. Old birthday cards
43. Broken toys
44. Happy Meal toys
45. Toys your kids never play with
46. Toys with missing pieces
47. Duplicates
48. Puzzles with missing pieces
49. Old books
50. Old swimsuits

This might just be the list that jumpstarts your cleaning and decluttering process. A quarantine is probably the best time to get this done because you're stuck at home anyway. You might as well make it a time to get all those projects done that you've been putting off. No better time to pull out that honey-do list and start checking things off, right?

Chapter 15

Faith Over Fear

I will preface this chapter by stating that I am a proud Christian and I believe in God as my creator. Therefore, when I speak of connecting to one's faith, I am speaking from my perspective as a Christian. You may tweak the content of this section by inserting your faith or belief if you wish, but I can only share from my perspective because I've never been invested in any other faith or religion.

*　　*　　*

It can be easy to start looking for reasons to no longer believe in God or find someone to blame for the bad things that happen in the world, but I firmly believe that God allows certain things to occur in our lives to wake us up and make us pay attention to what really matters.

That's why I feel it's more important now than ever to feed your faith and strengthen your relationship with a higher power. One thing I've noticed is that people will either draw closer to their faith in hard times or find reasons to abandon their faith. I encourage you to lean into your faith right now and deepen that connection. Doing this will not only put you in a more resourceful state to accomplish more and keep moving forward in your life, but it will also start activating blessings that might surprise you. Don't we all want to live a blessed life?

Here are 7 ways to activate your blessings through faith:

1. Expect great things in your life. If you want to abandon something right now, use this time to finally let go of those negative scripts that have been playing out in your head for years. They're not serving you. Start expecting better for yourself.

2. Speak great things into your life. Talk about your dreams and goals as if they are happening now or about to happen. Say things like, "I'm so grateful my family is drawing closer together, and my business is thriving." Or if it's not and you just can't convince yourself to say those things, say, "I'm so grateful to have been given another day to draw closer to my family, or to connect with amazing new people and grow my business."

3. Be grateful for great things you already have in your life. Wake up every day and say, "I'm so grateful for the breath

in my lungs and energy in my body to do the things I want to do and move the way I want to move. I'm grateful for everything that is working for my good right now." You can be grateful for your family, your home, your job, and your passions. Just find something.

4. Work toward great things in your life. Get up and set goals every day. Work toward accomplishing at least one goal and learning one new thing each day.

5. Plan great things in your life. Dream a little. Even though it seems miles away right now, create a vision board or journey board (as I call it) to inspire you to work toward those things, to do the activity it takes to make those dreams a reality. Plan dream vacations – learn a new language, write down an itinerary and places you'd like to visit, research the restaurants you want to dine in, etc.

6. Share great things in your life. Share your dreams with others. Share your blessings with others. Share what you're doing to make those dreams a reality. Share your journey along the way – the highs and lows, to attract others who can relate and possibly even join you on your journey.

7. Inspire great things in others. Post encouraging and inspiring things on social media. Send encouraging and inspiring text messages or emails to loved ones. Share accomplishments of your friends to inspire others to want to do the same.

It's not enough to speak an affirmation out loud every day. That alone will not move you toward your goals. You must believe it to your core, feel it in every fiber of your being, or else your brain thinks you're lying to it, and our brains won't allow us to lie to ourselves. They're not programmed to do that. What we tell ourselves must be true, according to our brains. So, start speaking your new truth. Start living your new truth. Your brain will start believing it and soon you'll become that which you seek to become.

Here are some ways to connect deeper to your faith, especially in a crisis:

- Pray every day – not just simple prayers, but deep, intentional prayers. Don't just pray for your family. Pray for strangers. Pray for your church and pastor. Pray for your government leaders. Pray for the President. We all need encouragement and guidance, especially in hard times. Don't forget to pray for the people who are in charge of our freedoms.

- Study your Bible and encouraging quotes every day. Do personal development every day to fill your mind with positive, empowering thoughts.

- Tithe. This is a controversial subject that may ruffle some feathers, but I truly feel that I live the blessed life I do, in part anyway, because I'm faithful in my relationship with God, and I tithe. Now, I personally don't believe tithing has to involve one giving money to a church, per se. I actually give my tithes to a charity that I am closely invested in and believe strongly in. One that has affected my loved ones in many ways. It's a cancer organization. That's where God led me to offer my monetary contributions.

- Spend some quiet time reflecting each day. You can meditate, pray, do yoga, whatever it is that calms your mind and body and puts you in an empowering and helpful state of being.

- Form a prayer group or Bible study group, to connect to and share your faith with others.
- Share your faith on social media, not in a way that condemns or judges others, but in a way that shows your pride and dedication. Show what God has done in your life.

Whatever it takes to keep you going in life every day, keep you moving the needle forward rather than sitting still or going backwards, lean into that and gain a deeper understanding and connection to it. That's what will get you through tough times, help you become a more compassionate mother, wife, and friend. We've all been affected by this situation in one way or another. This illness has equalized us as one world, showing no prejudice for any label we've given ourselves in our lifetimes. It has shown us the value of family. None of us are invincible or immune to death, illness, or catastrophe. We must take the time to slow down and appreciate the true gift of being alive, and strengthening our faith can ensure we do that.

Chapter 16

Making it Count

This book has served as a guide, thus far, to help people navigate many aspects of the world crisis we're going through. I started with addressing your mindset to accept and embrace the shift. I shared tips on how to set your family and household up for success to work from home or do school from home. I shared tips on how to manage the emotional, physical, and mental stress of being quarantined and practicing social distancing while also remaining a competent, functioning adult. I shared tips on how to save money on food costs and stretch your food supply in a dire situation. Tips on making money in a crisis and increasing your income by discovering a new side venture were also offered. I shared tips on how to protect your health and home by switching out the toxic elements. I even shared a few tips on how to lean into your faith and trust a higher power in this storm you're going through. All of those tips and strategies are going to serve you well in your day-to- day activities, to help you "get through" your every day.

However, it truly all comes down to a few simple questions:

- What do you want to have learned or accomplished at the end of this?
- What values and beliefs do you want your kids to gain through this experience?
- Who do you want to have become when this is all over?

Everything we experience in life is either a lesson, a blessing, or both. Sometimes we don't know what we're missing until it's gone. We don't know what value or purpose we truly offer until we share it with someone. We don't know just how disconnected we are, until we're forced to disconnect. We don't know the value of a dollar, until it's the one thing we need but don't have. We don't appreciate the true gift of working a job we love, until that job is no longer available.

This crisis has closed many doors for many people, but it has also opened many doors. More than ever people are looking into creating emergency funds, adding income sources, learning how to live on the basics, learning new skills, finding ways to contribute and serve others, and discovering new things about themselves. More parents are stepping into their power as a guiding force and central influence on their children. More families are coming together as one unit, as it should be.

What will this experience be for you? What story will this create for your family that's passed down for many generations from now?

- Did you create a new book, tool, or resource for others during this time?
- Did you teach people something new?
- Did you reach out and volunteer your time or expertise to enhance someone's life?
- Did you find a way to save or make money to better your family?
- Did you create a scrapbook or time capsule to document this moment in time with your kids?

Or:

- Did you simply discover a new TV show to binge watch?
- Did you sit around and share negative comments or posts on social media?
- Did you scroll through your friends' posts day after day wishing you had the guts or resources to do what they do or make something happen in the world?
- Did you "plan" to lose weight, write a book or song, reach a goal?
- Did you contribute to the mass media panic by sharing fake news or scare tactics?
- Did you condemn, be rude to, or laugh at others who were trying to share a resource or make a difference in the world, or for their families?

It's all about perspective. Some people will view this situation as a mere inconvenience in their life that they're going to "wait out." Others will view it as a wakeup call to get moving in their lives. Some will take it a step further and use this time to create amazing resources and memories with their loved ones.

I hope you find yourself in one of the two latter options. When we only focus on doing just enough to "get by" we're merely concerned about ourselves and our immediate needs. We're not impacting the world in any way by helping or empowering others. We're not solving any problems, we're simply adding to the existing problems. I hope this book has inspired you, at the very least, to get excited about the possibilities in your life right now.

Do something helpful. Do something different. Just do *something* that your future self or future generations will thank you for. Make this experience count. Make your life count.

Peace and blessings to you all. May you stay safe and well and come out on the other side of this as the best version of yourself.

Acknowledgements

First and foremost I want to thank God, my creator, for giving me the gift of writing; the gift of being able to break down complex – sometimes daunting concepts for people into manageable, applicable action steps; and the gift of building relationships with people. I've met some amazing people in my life, who have shaped the person I've become.

One of the most amazing people I've ever met is my husband, Denny. This man is truly my better half. He brings out the best in me, pushes me beyond my comfort level to achieve great things. In fact, he is responsible for inspiring me to write this book. He came to bed one night and kept pushing my buttons about doing something great amidst the world crisis going on right now. He spoke confidence into me and told me I had a gift inside of me that the world needed to experience now more than ever. At first I was annoyed by all this, but when I took the time to embrace it, the words flowed from my heart like a raging river. I couldn't stop it if I tried. I am so thankful to have this man in my life who truly is my best friend.

I'm also thankful to my children, who have always been my reason for everything I do. They're my inspiration to want to constantly strive to be a better mom, wife, and person in general. If nothing else, I hope I've taught them to always be kind to others and help where you can, just like my parents taught me. I want them to know that kindness will take you to places in your life that you can only dream about. It can open doors sometimes that money, prestige, and power can't. It's the most important part of being alive. I hope when I'm gone from this world, they see that I always did my best to ensure they became competent, confident, contributing humans because that's what life is truly about.

I want to thank my sisters and my parents who have always cheered me on, even when they thought my ideas were crazy or impractical. We definitely have our differences, but I know they want the best for me and they'll always be there for me when I need them. Whether it's watching my Facebook LIVES, reading my books, or inspiring me to create new resources, I know they support me and are always in my corner.

Finally, I want to thank my friend, Beth Hale, for her unwavering friendship from the moment I met her several years ago as I was just starting my publishing journey. She has been a critique partner and great friend every step of the way, and she always inspires me to become a better writer every time I read one of her books. She is also responsible for proofreading this book at a moment's notice, so I could get this message out to the world quickly and effectively. I can't thank her enough for that.

I appreciate every single person who took the time to read this book, whether you agreed with all of my tips and strategies or not. It takes all kinds of kinds to make the world go 'round, and I appreciate every person I come in contact with because they either teach me something about the world or something about myself. For that, I'm always grateful.

Peace and blessings to you and your family from mine.

About Traci Sanders

Traci Sanders is work-from-home mom of three and proud Nonna of one. Her experience as a mom and childcare provider for more than twenty years inspired her to pen several books about parenting and caring for children professionally. Sanders is also a public speaker who educates women on topics related to health, relationships, and finances, empowering them to become the best versions of themselves.

Fresh Ink Group
Independent Multi-media Publisher

Fresh Ink Group / Push Pull Press

&

Hardcovers
Softcovers
All Ebook Platforms
Audiobooks
Worldwide Distribution

&

Indie Author Services
Book Development, Editing, Proofing
Graphic/Cover Design
Video/Trailer Production
Website Creation
Social Media Management
Writing Contests
Writers' Blogs
Podcasts

&

Authors
Editors
Artists
Experts
Professionals

&

FreshInkGroup.com
info@FreshInkGroup.com
Twitter: @FreshInkGroup
Facebook.com/FreshInkGroup
LinkedIn: Fresh Ink Group

Fresh Ink Group

Right At Home
A parent's guide to choosing quality child care

Award-winning Early Childhood Educator reveals the pros and cons of all child care settings.

Traci M. Sanders

LITTLE SPONGES
TEACHING TODDLERS THE BASIC CONCEPTS

FROM AWARD-WINNING
EARLY CHILDHOOD EDUCATOR

TRACI M. SANDERS

"Sanders succinctly explains when a baby is physiologically ready for potty training and gives readers a fairly detailed plan."
-Holly Scudero, San Diego Book Review

Welcome to
POOP CAMP
The Truth, the Whole Truth,
and Nothing but the Truth
about Potty Training

Traci M. Sanders

JUST LIKE HOME

Adventures in
Family Child Care
Written by: Traci M Sanders Illustrated by: Kristy Moore

Lightning Source UK Ltd.
Milton Keynes UK
UKHW021450070620
364500UK00002B/370